INTENTIONAL GRATITUDE

52 Ways to Discover the Blessings in Your Life

By Betty Everitt Lochner

2019

Arietta Press

Olympia, Washington

INTENTIONAL GRATITUDE
52 Ways to Discover the Blessings in Your Life
By Betty Everitt Lochner

Copyright ©2019 Cornerstone Coaching & Training, LLC
All rights reserved.

Published by Arietta Press
1827 Arietta Ave SE, Olympia, WA 98501

No part of this book may be reproduced or transmitted in any form or by any means, electronic or mechanical, including photocopying, recording or by any information storage and retrieval system, without the express written permission of the publisher, except for the inclusion of brief quotations in a review. To obtain permission to reproduce go to www.cornerstone-ct.com or write to the publisher.

Ordering Information

Publications can be ordered direct from:

betty@cornerstone-ct.com

Quantity sales: special discounts are available on quantity purchases by organizations, associations, colleges and other groups.

INTENTIONAL GRATITUDE is also available on Amazon.

ISBN: 9781087496542

Photographs by Carolyn Cummins - Shootin' For Fun Photography

A note from the photographer:

Hello! My name is Carolyn Cummins and I have been *Shootin' For Fun* most of my life! My focus (pun intended) is on scenic, landscape, nature, wildlife and macro of flowers and insects. I love being outdoors and capturing anything that catches my eye. God's amazing creation that surrounds us truly brings me joy!

Website: www.shootinforfun.com
Email: shootinforfun@gmail.com

This journal belongs to:

_____

If found, please contact me at:

_____

The date I began:

_____

For my grandbabies - Azriel, Moses and Addison.

I am so very grateful to be your NaNa.

INTRODUCTION

Intentional [in'ten(t)SH(ə)n(ə)l]
ADJECTIVE - Done on purpose; deliberate.
synonyms: deliberate · conscious · done on purpose · intended · planned · meant · considered · studied

Gratitude ['gradə,t(y)o͞od]
NOUN - The quality of being thankful; readiness to show appreciation for and to return kindness.
synonyms: gratefulness · thankfulness · appreciation · recognition · acknowledgment · graciousness · grace

Welcome to an opportunity to change your life

We live in a stressful world where it is easy to feel overwhelmed. The prevalent use of the latest technology - generally designed to give us more connection - can instead leave us feeling a disconnection from each other and from ourselves.

There is a way to reset, refresh and give ourselves some grace and perspective. It comes through the practice of intentional gratitude.

Intentional gratitude is a way for us to discover and acknowledge the goodness in our lives, whether tangible or intangible. Through gratitude, we learn to recognize that the source of that goodness lies at least partially outside of ourselves. As a result, gratitude helps us connect to something larger than ourselves — whether to other people, nature, or a higher power.

When we practice gratitude, we reap a multitude of positive benefits including a healthier mindset, more confidence, better health, less stress and stronger relationships. Here's what research has to say about gratitude:

- **Gratitude makes you more optimistic.** People who are more focused on the things they are grateful for than on the things that upset them are more optimistic and happier with their lives. They also have fewer visits to physicians (Emmons, University of California, Davis and McCullough, University of Miami).

- **Optimistic people live longer.** People who tend to be optimistic are more likely than others to live to be 85 years old or more (University of Boston, 2019).

- **Gratitude improves physical health.** Grateful people experience fewer aches and pains and report that they feel healthier overall. (Personality and Individual Differences, 2012).

- **Gratitude improves psychological health.** Practicing gratitude reduces the amount of negative emotions we experience including anger, envy, resentment, regret, and even depression (multiple studies by Robert A. Emmons, Ph.D.)

- **Gratitude helps you sleep better and longer.** (Applied Psychology: Health and Well-Being, 2012).

- **Gratitude improves your self-esteem and helps you perform better.** (Journal of Applied Sport Psychology, 2014).

- **Gratitude improves relationships.** Individuals who take time to express gratitude for their partner not only feel more positive toward the other person but also feel more comfortable expressing concerns about their relationship, an important component of a healthy relationship (Kubacka and colleagues, 2011).

- **Gratitude is a workplace motivator.** When managers use gratitude to say thank you to their employees for their efforts, they motivate them to work harder (University of Wharton, 2010).

- **Benefits to adolescents.** In adolescents, gratitude has been shown to reduce materialism and increase generosity (Journal of Positive Psychology, 2018). Another study concluded that gratitude can lead to healthier eating in young people (Journal of Experimental Psychology, 2019).

- **Benefits to the elderly.** In the elderly, gratitude has been found to reduce loneliness (Gonzaga University, 2019).

We have much be grateful for

We live in a culture of overwhelming abundance and blessings. In many ways, gratitude is simply the practice of realizing we have enough. Think about this:

- If you have food in your refrigerator, clothes on your back, a roof over your head and a place to sleep then **you are richer than 75 percent** of this world.
- If you have money in the bank, in your wallet, and spare change in a dish someplace, then you are among the **top eight per cent** of the world's wealthy.
- If you make $34,000 a year, you are in the **1% of the richest people** in the world.

The power to choose

*Your life comes down to your decisions.
If you change your decisions, you'll change your life.* ~ Mel Robbins

Gratitude isn't an automatic response. It's a learned behavior. We can choose whether to embrace it or not.

This book is designed to give you different ideas and ways to practice gratitude. It is my hope that you will use them to begin claiming your own personal practice of intentional gratitude.

The 52-week challenge

Building a lifelong habit of practicing daily gratitude will take commitment and discipline.

If you take the challenge, you will build the habit of intentional gratitude by writing and reflecting daily for 52-weeks.

Why Journaling is Important

Studies show that the act of writing things down helps us build habits and visual messaging (also known as sketch noting or doodling) improves retention. Compared with writing alone, adding drawings to notes to represent concepts, terms, and relationships has a significant effect on memory and learning. (Wammes, Meade, & Fernandes, 2016).

Success Tips

- Starting today, pick a day of the week. That day, you will start a new gratitude prompt. Work on that prompt every day you possibly can during the week. For each consecutive week, start a different prompt for the week.

- Getting comfortable with the uncomfortable is the key to growth! Spend the entire week on each prompt before moving on, whether you love that one or not.

- Start with the first prompt and end with the last one. After that, it's okay to skip around or go back and do a prompt over. Some prompts are more challenging than others, but the effort of following through and completing them all will be well worth it.

- You may find a prompt you love. When you do, own it and continue beyond the week, but make sure you also continue doing the new prompts until you've completed them all.

- Let your creative side loose! Use your favorite pens, colors, and doodles to express thoughts, emotions and your gratitude in this journal. Have some fun and make it yours.

    Note: Many of these gratitude prompts are also excellent activities to do with someone else – a partner or children at mealtime, or on special occasions such as birthdays and Thanksgiving with your extended family and friends.

The work you put into practicing the skill of regular intentional gratitude will pay huge dividends for you both at work and at home. If you take personal action and work on one prompt every week for 52 weeks, you will build a strong foundation of intentional gratitude habits. I guarantee that you'll see some amazing results in your life.

Let's do this.

cat
friends sunsets dog
vacation
church sunshine
health paycheck career
laughter
slippers children music
freedom car
house family
food partner
wine

It's important to make gratitude a habit because your habits create your life.
~ Sandy Harper, author

1. Count Your Blessings

Brainstorm everything that comes to mind that you are thankful for. Compile your list here and add to it each day this week. When you are done, have some fun with your list – consider making a word cloud to save or share on www.wordclouds.com

Continue brainstorming more blessings......

...and even more...

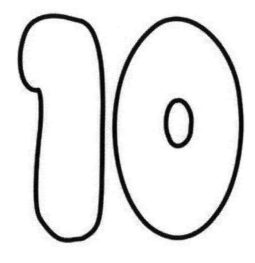

Piglet noticed that even though he had a very small heart; it could hold a rather large amount of gratitude. ~ AA Milne, Winnie the Pooh

2. Top 10 List

Look over your list of blessings that you compiled in prompt #1 (complete that list first if you haven't already). Circle your top 10. Record them on the next pages.

The Top 10 Things I am grateful for are:

1	
2	
3	
4	
5	

6	
7	
8	
9	
10	

Make a copy of your list and put it somewhere where you will see it every day.

Give Thanks with a Grateful Heart — 1 Thessalonians 5:18

Happiness is the result of praise and thanksgiving, of faith, of acceptance; a quiet tranquil realization of the love of God. ~ White Eagle

3. Meditation and Prayer

The practice of meditation and prayer is powerful. It focuses our thoughts on something outside of ourselves. The benefits are proven regardless of what your personal faith is.

The act of meditation and prayer can trigger and release brain chemicals that make you feel good, including oxytocin. It also calms us and give us hope.

If you haven't experienced meditation or prayer, try 10 minutes a day. If you already meditate or pray regularly, consider increasing the focus and time spent this week.

Here are some ways to start:

- Clear your mind. Breathe in from your nose and out through your mouth. Focus on the present moment and what you are grateful for.

- Give thanks and praise.

- Consider your own needs.

- Consider others.

Resource:
https://www.nbcnews.com/better/health/your-brain-prayer-meditation-ncna812376

Write about your reflections, feelings, and thoughts about the place of mediation and prayer in your life.

*Meditation is a life long gift.
It's something you can call on anytime.*
~ Paul McCartney

The most precious things of life are near at hand.
~ John Burroughs

4. Experience Awe

What is something that you have experienced in the past that gave you a sense of awe? Examples could include majestic natural environments, a sunset, stargazing, or observing a full moon, viewing artistic work, listening to music that moves you, or examples of human compassion and kindness.

Write about your reflections from that experience.

Spend the week seeking out and experiencing awe in your everyday life. What gives you a sense of peace, or goosebumps? Pick out at least one thing each day that you see as beautiful – that gives you a sense of awe.

Resource: https://forge.medium.com/the-natural-cure-for-burnout-is-profound-and-utter-awe-bfa9f6b3e2d1

This day is a journey, this very moment an adventure.
 ~ Rebecca Pavlenko

5. Capture Moments

Take a photo each day of something that you appreciate – for example something that makes you laugh or smile, or makes you feel lucky and loved. If you take more than one picture each day, pick out your favorite.

Write about what you photograph each day, and why you chose it.

Daily Photo Log
What did you choose and what's the story it tells?

Day 1	
Day 2	
Day 3	

Day 4	
Day 5	
Day 6	
Day 7	

I AM ENOUGH

What is life for? It is for you.
~ Abraham Maslow

6. Be Kind to Yourself

As you are exploring gratitude in your life, don't forget to be kind to yourself. There is only one unique you, and **you are enough**! You don't need to be anyone else. Just be you.

Do you like and appreciate yourself? If not, what's stopping you?

Do a bit of self-reflection and self-awareness. Work on thinking daily positive thoughts about yourself.

List something each day that you like about yourself. I am...

GRATEFUL thankful BLESSED

We are most alive in those moments when our hearts are conscious of our treasures. ~ Thorton Wilder

7. Daily Blessings

Before you go to bed each night, shift your thinking from what you are worried about to counting all your blessings. It will make you more likely to stay asleep and not wake up thinking of a problem.

Spend 10 minutes before you go to bed each night to write down everything you are thankful for today.

What I'm thankful for today...

Day 1	
Day 2	
Day 3	

Day 4	
Day 5	
Day 6	
Day 7	

Now, sleep well.

If you want to feel rich, just count all the gifts you have that money can't buy.
~ Proverb

8. Gratitude Jar

When something happens that you are grateful for this week, write it down on a slip of paper and put it in a jar. At the end of the week – take them all out and read them aloud.

This can be an individual or family exercise. You can collect things you are grateful for or appreciate about each other and then monthly or annually, pull them out and reflect on your blessings.

Write in the jar all the positive words you can think of that describe your life.

Today I live in the quiet, joyous expectation of good.
~ Ernest Holmen

9. Sounds of Gratitude

Take a few minutes at the beginning of your day to go outside or take a walk and listen for sounds of gratitude – music, birds…try to get away from the noise of traffic and horns and busyness. Listen for the pleasing sounds around you.

Really listen. What do you hear? What do those sounds represent to you?

List all the words that describe the daily sounds of gratitude you heard.

*The sun does not shine for a few trees and flowers,
but for the wide world's joy, including yours.* ~ Henry Ward Beecher

10. Mindful Walk

Each day this week, carve out time to take a walk outside. It doesn't have to be long – even 5-10 minutes will work.

While you're walking, notice details around you. What plants are visible? What color is your neighbor's house? Look up and say hello to everyone you pass. Write about your experiences.

Let us be grateful to people who make us happy;
they are the charming gardeners who make our souls blossom.
~ Marcel Proust

11. Reconnect

Think of the people in your life that you like and appreciate but haven't talked to for a while.

Call, email, or text them and just let them know you are thinking about them.

Think about how you can make time to reconnect more often with people you don't see in your daily life.

List the people you want to reconnect with here. Then reach out to them.

This is the gift – to have the wonderful capacity to appreciate again and again, freshly and naively, the basic good of life, with awe, pleasure, wonder, and even ecstasy. ~ Abraham Maslow

12. Joyful Memories

Think of a joyful memory. Maybe the birth of a child, a wedding, or another special time. What comes to your mind? Who was involved?

Write in as much detail as you can what the experience was and how it made you feel. You can choose to focus on one experience and add detail each day, or several different experiences.

How did it feel both physically and emotionally?

Blessed

Joy is a light that fills you with hope and faith and love.
~ Adela Rodgers St. Johns

13. What's Going Right

Notice the small details of what's going right for you this week – for example, you found a great parking spot, you had a fun evening with friends, your name was chosen for a door prize…

Write about them and how they made you feel.

thankful & grateful

*He is a wise man who does not grieve for the things which he has not,
but rejoices for those which he has.* – Epictetus

14. Back to Basics

Take time to notice more of what you do have then what you don't have.

Write down three things each day that you may take for granted – such as clean running water, transportation, garbage services, paved roads….

Day 1

Day 2

Day 3

 Day 4

 Day 5

Day 6

Day 7

When eating bamboo plants,
remember the farmer who planted them. ~ Chinese Proverb

15. Food for Thought

Before you eat each meal this week, think about where the food came from. Give thanks to whatever part of the process you feel the most connection with.

Then, take your time to savor every bite – the texture, the flavor, the smell. Reflect on your mealtime experiences.

What does it look, smell, feel and taste like?

Fully enjoy the experience and see how long you can make it last.

The way to develop the best that is in a person is by appreciation and encouragement. ~ Charles Schwab

16. Thank Someone

Go out of your way to thank someone each day this week who has done something for you that has made your life better. It can be as simple as bringing your coffee to you, smiling when there is nothing to smile about, etc. or something more significant.

Choose a family member, colleague, your barista, a stranger, or anyone who you are grateful for this week. Tell them *thank you* – describe what they did for you and be as specific as you can.

Who was it each day and what did you say?

Day 1

Day 2

Day 3

Day 4

Day 5

Day 6

Day 7

There is no joy without gratitude. ~ Brene' Brown

17. Revisit a Keepsake

Read a card, note, letter, poem, section of a favorite book, or other treasure you've saved. Write down an excerpt. Why do you like it? Why have you saved it?

Continue throughout the week – what treasures have you found?

Never squander an opportunity to tell someone you love or appreciate them.
~ Kelly Ann Rothaus

18. Pay it Forward

Do something nice for someone. Do a favor, bring someone their favorite drink, or do a chore without being asked.

Find at least one nice thing you can do for no special reason each day.

Who did you choose, and what did you do for them?

grateful ♡

When you cease from labor fill up your time in reading, meditation and prayer; and while your hands are laboring, let your heart be employed, as much as possible, in divine thoughts. ~ David Brainerd

19. Be Silent

Do something in complete silence each day that you find nourishing to your soul. Take a walk, meditate, have a cup of tea, stare out a window at a pretty view. Relish and thoroughly enjoy the experience without distraction or interruption.

Reflect and write about your experiences.

How did it feel to intentionally take time to be still? Did it get easier each day?

*Remember those ships who pass through your day, touching your life just once,
sending you into a better direction than your life was headed.*
~ Michelle C Ustaszeski

20. Important People

This week make a list of at least 5 people who have made a significant difference in your life; who have had a positive influence on you or brought out the best in you.

Who are they, what did they do, how did that make you feel?

♥

♥

Every single day do something that makes your heart sing. ~ Marcia Wieder

21. Joy of the Day

What brought you joy and happiness today – big or small? Write down three good and joyful things that happen each day of the week.

Simply grateful

The real gift of gratitude is that the more grateful you are, the more present you become. ~ Robert Holden

22. Be Present

Focus on being present in your life this week – in each single moment.

Try to stay away from what I call "future tripping" (*I'll be happy when…*). When you catch yourself thinking about how something will be better in the future, stop and reframe your thoughts to what you are thankful only for today.

Reflect on when you caught yourself future tripping. How easy was it to change your focus back to the present?

Someone is sitting in the shade today because someone planted a tree a long time ago. ~ Warren Buffett

23. Reflect on Your Success

Write about something that leaves you feeling satisfied or accomplished. Allow yourself the pleasure of basking in it. Be grateful for the opportunity and for the success. Celebrate it!

As you think of your successes, describe what they were. Be as specific as you can.

Who are you grateful for in helping you succeed?

Optional activity: Start a Success File or Notebook of things that you have accomplished or have been recognized for – a note from your boss, a letter of congratulations, a certificate or award. Add to it regularly. Then, when you are having a rough day, you can go back and be reminded of and be grateful for your past successes!

the root of
joy
is gratefulness

Gratitude is the healthiest of all human emotions. The more you express gratitude for what you have, the more likely you will have even more to express gratitude for. ~ Zig Ziglar

24. Simple Joy

List simple, everyday things that make you happy. For example, the smell of coffee in the morning, your dog wagging his tail when you enter the room, your flower garden.... Start your list here.

Pay attention to the things you don't normally put any thought into – even a chore like washing the dishes, doing laundry, sitting in traffic... Look for something in the experience that is enjoyable or beautiful. Continue to write about your daily ordinary experiences.

What simple things give you joy?

All the great blessings of my life are present in my thoughts today. ~ Phoebe Cary

25. Create White Space

Your brain needs a rest.

This week concentrate on getting some down time. What can you let go of to make more time for yourself and reflection?

Use these pages to doodle.

A letter is never ill-timed; it never interrupts. Instead it waits for us to find the opportune minute, the quiet moment to savor the message. There is an element of timelessness about letter writing. ~ Lois Wyse

26. Write a Letter

Review your list of important people from action prompt #20.

Write a letter of appreciation to at least one person on your list. Tell them what he or she specifically did that still affects your life. Send the letter.

Try some draft letters here –
brainstorm what you want to say and how to best say it.

Gratitude

It is not joy that makes us grateful; it is gratitude that makes us joyful.
~ David Steindl-Rast

27. Self-Care

Take time to practice putting your self-care first. Which of the following areas are you doing well in and which can you improve upon?

- Sleep
- Exercise
- Rest and relaxation
- Social connections (with the people you like/love)
- Manage stress (do you ask for help when you need it?)
- Gratitude

What is your plan for increasing or improving your self-care?

We tend to forget that happiness doesn't come as a result of getting something we don't have, but rather of recognizing and appreciating what we do have.
~ Frederick Koenig

28. Pause and Appreciate

When you shift your focus to the positive parts of your day, it trains your brain to shift away from focusing on the negative parts and what is causing you stress in the moment.

Each day this week, list the positive things that happened. Then pause and appreciate the details of each.

List them here in as much detail as you can.

Day 1

Day 2

Day 3

Day 4

Day 5

Day 6

Day 7

The state of your life is nothing more than a reflection of your state of mind.

~ Wayne Dyer

29. Self-Reflection

Check in with yourself. How are you feeling? Happy, tired, sad, content, stressed....?

Whatever you feel, give yourself permission to fully experience your emotions.

Write all about it. If the feeling is negative, imagine a more positive space. What does the act of writing about your mood have on it?

Check in with yourself daily....

Thankfulness is the beginning of gratitude. Gratitude is the completion of thankfulness. Thankfulness may consist merely of words. Gratitude is shown in acts. ~ Henri Frederick Amiel

30. Laser Focus

Take a few minutes to write down everything you appreciate about this very moment. Right now, wherever you are.

How does it feel to laser focus on what you appreciate?

Do this at least one time each day this week.

What did you discover?

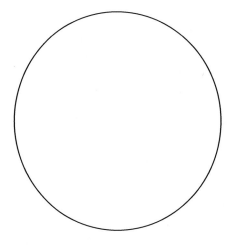

Live life as if everything is rigged in your favor. ~ Rumi

31. Circle of Gratitude

We can easily be grateful for all the tangible blessings that have come our way in life, but it's important to also be grateful for all that *hasn't* happened — for all the bad things that could have happened but didn't.

The distance between them happening and not happening is grace and gratitude.

Use the concentric circles on the next pages to reflect on how there are blessings in our daily struggles.

Small circle: Write down the small things you are grateful for.
Middle circle: Write down the things you worried about, but that didn't happen.
Outer area: Write down the hidden blessings and learning found in the struggles you have faced.

Do you have any additional insights?

No one can make you feel inferior without your consent. ~ Eleanor Roosevelt

32. Change Your Mindset

Take time this week to think about your mindset. Do you have a positive, growth mindset?

In other words, are you looking to learn and grow from situations in your life?

Fixed Mindset

> A person's abilities and qualities are set
> Capabilities have a predetermined limit

Growth Mindset

> Basic qualities can be cultivated through effort
> True potential is unknown

Resource: *Mindset: How we Can Learn to Fulfill our Potential* by Carol S Dweck, Ph.D.

Growth Mindset Thinking

INSTEAD OF….	TRY THINKING….
I'm not good at this.	What am I missing?
I give up.	I'll use a different strategy.
I can't make this any better.	I can always improve.
This is too hard.	This may take some time.
I made a mistake.	Mistakes help me learn.
I just can't do this.	I am going to train my brain.
I'll never be that smart.	I will learn how to do this.
Plan A didn't work.	There's always Plan B.
My friend can do it.	I will learn from them.

What you feed your mind, you feed your life.
~ Kemi Sogunle

What can you do differently to change develop more of a growth mindset?

Creativity takes courage. ~ Henri Matisse

33. Be Creative

What is a creative outlet you enjoy? Take time to channel your creative energy. Put on your favorite songs and sing along, dance around the kitchen, create art, garden….

What creative energy did you tap into this week?

*I would maintain that thanks are the highest form of thought,
and that gratitude is happiness doubled by wonder.* ~ Gilbert C. Chesterton

34. Write a Note of Gratitude

You can make yourself happier and nurture your relationship with another person by writing a thank-you letter expressing your enjoyment and appreciation of that person's impact on your life.

Discover the power of the handwritten note. Send one to a different person each day this week. Note: If handwritten is not feasible, then email/text is a good second option.

Day 1

Day 2

Day 3

Day 4

Day 5

Day 6

Day 7

The mind is everything. What you think, you become. ~ Buddha

35. Slow Down

During at least one activity each day, slow it down. Don't multitask. Whatever you are doing, do only that one thing.

Be careful of distractions and interruptions. How was the experience different from how you normally approach tasks throughout your day?

When you are going about your day, strive to stay in the moment – Look up and out (and that often means putting your phone away) – at the grocery store, getting a pedicure, etc.

How does slowing down change your experiences?

Gratitude

When I started counting my blessings, my whole life turned around.
 ~ Willie Nelson

36. Wall of Gratitude

Use a wall, flip chart, chalk board, poster board, or white board and write in the center of it the word **Gratitude.**

Now take sticky notes and each day write down at least one thing that you are grateful for each day. Leave it up for a while and count your blessings.

Note: This also works great as a work team or family exercise.

Write about your sticky note experience.

oOo   oOo   oOo   oOo

oOo

The most important things in life aren't things. ~ Anthony D'Angelo

37. Life Influencers

Seek out a teacher or boss who had a positive influence on you and tell them via email, letter, or even better – in person! What will you say and how will you say it? Then, write about the experience.

It is not joy that makes us grateful, it is gratitude that makes us joyful.
~ Brother David Steindle-Rost

38. Bless Someone

Do something tangible for those you appreciate. For example, bring treats to work or leave a note or treat in your partner's briefcase.

Or simply write or say *Thank You*. Bless someone different each day this week.

Day 1

Day 2

Day 3

Day 4

Day 5

Day 6

Day 7

Wear gratitude like a cloak and it will feed every corner of your life. ~ Rumi

39. First Things First

Try out a new morning routine that helps you start your day with gratitude and wellness.

Here are some ideas to start with. Modify or add to it throughout the week to see what works best for you.

    1, Express Gratitude.

    2. Set your intentions for the Day - What do you plan to do? What are your goals?).

    3. Breathe deeply - take 5 long deep breaths in and out.

    4. Stretch your body - reach to the ceiling, then down to your toes.

    5. Think of things that make you smile.

    6. Forgive yourself for yesterday's mistakes. Instead reflect on what you learned and move on.

What morning routines did you try out?

Be Grateful

> Now is no time to think of what you do not have.
> Think of what you can do with what there is.
> ~ Ernest Hemingway

40. Examine a Personal Challenge

Write about a problem you are experiencing in your life. Look for the positive. Keep going until you find the gratitude in the situation you are going through. Try thinking about all the ways it could be worse, or what the positive outcome will be when it's resolved.

Not what we have, but what we enjoy, constitutes our abundance.
~ John Petit-Senn

41. Less is More

We are an abundant culture. Think about it: how many coats or shoes do you have vs. how many do you realistically need?

Do you have more than you need?

What do you have that you are ready to release to bless someone else?

Now find a way to bless someone with your abundance by gifting it or donating it to a family less fortunate through a charity. Some examples are the food bank, Habitat for Humanity, your local women's or homeless shelter, or another agency that will use it to help someone who needs help.

What did you choose to let go of? Who did you bless with it?

Stretch out your hand and receive the world's wide gift of joy, appreciation and beauty. ~ Corinne Roosevelt Robinson

42. Rest and Reflect

Take time each day to rest and reflect. Spend it however you wish with a focus on gratitude.

Write about what you choose to do each day.

Gracious words are a honeycomb, sweet to the soul and healing to the bones.
~ Proverbs 16:24

43. Messages to Yourself

Talk to yourself like someone you love every day.

Concentrate on talking positively to yourself this week. Forgive yourself for thinking negative thoughts or beating yourself up and just talk nice to yourself.

How does that feel? How can you make positive self-talk a part of your daily life?

Celebrate ♥

Your future depends on many things, but mostly yourself. ~ Frank Tyger

43. Congratulate yourself

Write about what happens this week that leaves you feeling satisfied or accomplished. Describe what it was. What did you get done? What was your part in the success?

You have no cause for anything but gratitude and joy.
~ Buddha

44. Sunrise, Sunset

This week go out of your way to watch a sunrise on at least one day, and a sunset on another.

How hard was it to make this happen? Was it worth it?

☆ ☆ ☆ ☆ ☆

You. ♡

Focus on the positive experiences and you'll have more of those.
~ LeAura Alderson

45. Positive Affirmations

Give yourself some positive affirmations. Use one or more of the following and say them out loud to yourself daily. Add additional affirmations that are meaningful to your life.

- I am Worthy

- I am Strong

- I am Courageous

- I am Beautiful

- I am Willing

- I am Smart

- I am Loved

- I am Enough

- I am Confident

- I am Abundant

- I am Accepting

What other affirmations can you add to the list?

As we express our gratitude, we must never forget that the highest appreciation is not to utter words, but to live by them. ~ John F. Kennedy

46. Turn it Around

Pick a person in your life that you may be having a disagreement with or are currently experiencing a struggle in your relationship.

Write about why you are grateful for them despite your differences.

It's not the years in your life that count, It's the life in your years. ~ Abe Lincoln

47. Move

Exercise and movement - even for just a few minutes - has a positive effect on your mind.

Each day this week take time to move - bike, dance, do yoga, or take a walk with a friend. Be intentional and do it each day.

Reflect on how it made you feel.

When we focus on our gratitude, the tide of disappointment goes out and the tide of love rushes in. ~ Kirstin Armstrong (Olympia Athlete)

48. Love What You Do

Make a list of all the activities you love to do.

Which ones do you do regularly? Which ones can you do more often? Pick out three that you don't do regularly and do them this week. Write about what you did.

Day 1

Day 2

Day 3

Day 4

Day 5

Day 6

Day 7

Never squander an opportunity to tell someone you love or appreciate them.
~ Kelly Ann Rothaus

49. Turn Positive Thoughts into Action

Building and sustaining gratitude in your daily life contributes to developing emotional maturity. Finding joy beyond ourselves and sharing our abundance with others is gratitude in action.

Spend this week reflecting on how you feel you have changed or grown through building daily gratitude into your life.

Our positive thoughts turn into our feelings.

Our feelings turn into positive action.

Thoughts → Feelings

Feelings → Actions

●

From small beginnings come great things. ~ Proverb

50. Try Something New

What is something you've always wanted to do but haven't? This week think of something new you can try. It can be as simple as making a playlist of your favorite inspirational songs or reading a book on a skill you want to get better at, or a place you want to travel to.

Get out of your routine and do something different – try a different route to work, eat something different, try a new exercise class.

Write about your new experiences.

And I think to myself……*

51. What a Wonderful World

*Listen to the song *What a Wonderful World*, recorded by Louis Armstrong or John Legend. You can also look for other songs or ways you feel inspired.

Then, each day write down at least three positive things going on in your life that you aren't directly responsible for.

Day 1

Day 2

Day 3

Day 4

Day 5

Day 6

Day 7

gratitude changes everything

Love the life you live; Live the life you love. ~ Bob Marley

52. Love the Life You Live

Review your entries in this journal – what are the themes that have emerged for you?

Take time to reflect and choose the gratitude prompts that resonated well with you and/or worked best for you.

Which ones will you use regularly to continue to make gratitude a daily habit?

How will you continue to discover the role of intentional gratitude in your life?

Conclusion

Congratulations on investing the time and energy in developing some intentional gratitude habits!

I encourage you to continue to use the prompts that resonated with you. Do them daily and reflect in a gratitude journal. The results will continue to be transforming.

Continue your Learning

For more information, resources, and communication tips, visit: www.cornerstone-ct.com

To give feedback on this journal, schedule an individual consultation, coaching, presentation, workshop, or training contact: betty@cornerstone-ct.com

I'd love to hear from you!

Other books by Betty Everitt Lochner

- *Dancing with Strangers*
- *52 Communication Tips*
- *Gladie's Gift*

Quantity sales: special discounts are available on quantity purchases by organizations, associations, colleges and other groups.

Intentional Gratitude is also available on Amazon.

Bibliography and Recommended reading:

Brene' Brown. *Dare to Lead*

Dweck, Carol S., Ph.D. *Mindset: How we Can Learn to Fulfill our Potential*

Huffington, Arianna. *Thrive: The Third Metric to Redefining Success and Creating a Life of Well-Being, Wisdom, and Wonder*

Lochner, Betty. *52 Communication Tips*

Morin, Amy. *13 Things Mentally Strong People Don't Do*

Pasricha, Neil. *The Book of Awesome*

Robbins, Mel. *The Five-Second Rule*

Silverstein, Shel. *The Giving Tree*

Sorell, **Traci**. *We Are Grateful: Otsaliheliga*

Voscamp, Ann. *One Thousand Gifts: A Dare to Live Fully Right Where You Are*

'Thank you' is the best prayer that anyone could say. I say that one a lot. Thank you expresses extreme gratitude, humility, and understanding. ~ Alice Walker

Made in the USA
Lexington, KY
18 September 2019